QUEEN MAGIC

**Freddie Mercury Tribute
and
Brian May Interview**

By JIM O'DONNELL

CS

First Edition, August, 2013
ISBN-13: 978-1491235393
ISBN-10: 149123539X

Websites:
CenterStageMedia.us.com
CenterStageMedia.uk.com
CenterStageMediaCanada.com

Permissions/Subsidiary Rights/Media/Corrections/Messages:
Permissions: permissions@centerstagemedia.us.com
Reprints: reprints@centerstagemedia.us.com
Translation: translationrights@centerstagemedia.us.com
International: interrights@centerstagemedia.us.com
Other Rights: subrights@centerstagemedia.us.com
Media Inquiries: publicity@centerstagemedia.us.com
Corrections: corrections@centerstagemedia.us.com
Messages for author: jimodonnell@centerstagemedia.us.com

Special order inquiries (bulk orders, school orders, etc.):
U.S.: specialorders@centerstagemeida.us.com
U.K.: specialorders@centerstagemedia.uk.com

Publisher's U.S. Address:
CreateSpace Independent Publishing Platform
4900 LaCross Road
North Charleston, SC 29406

This book is dedicated to

Shannon,

my forever-loving daughter.

ACKNOWLEDGMENTS

The author wishes to thank Vincent Velasquez, president of HurricaneProductions.com, for his assistance. Hurricane Productions is a communications and entertainment company. The company's production and marketing work has been invaluable.

The author also wishes to acknowledge that this is not an official Queen product. *Queen Magic* was designed, formatted and released independently of Queen or anyone directly associated with Queen. No endorsement of this book from Queen or its associates is stated or implied.

Queen Gets Royal Treatment In Language of *Queen Magic*

The English rock band Queen gets the royal treatment from the English language in *Queen Magic*. The world class group is brought to life through amazingly vivid detail in two pieces of writing from longtime rock music author Jim O'Donnell.

The first piece is O'Donnell's landmark review of 1992's Freddie Mercury Tribute Concert at Wembley Stadium, London, watched on TV by an estimated billion people. In the process of telling the story of the show, the piece tells the story of Queen in language fit for a king. Written in a lively style with many comic touches, the review steps far beyond center-stage and into the realm of fresh insight.

The second piece is a deeply felt interview with Queen guitarist Brian May that O'Donnell conducted shortly after Freddie Mercury's death in 1991. The interview is a genuine, personal glimpse of the guitarist's feelings about his lead-singer and his band.

According to the late Ray Coleman, former Editor-in-Chief of *Melody Maker,* "Jim O'Donnell's extraordinary piece on the Mercury farewell concert is the best writing I've ever seen on Freddie or, for that matter, on Queen."

All in all, *Queen Magic* uses the written word to discover and reveal the essence of this legendary band.

About the Author

Jim O'Donnell is a longtime music writer whose work is in the Rock 'n' Roll Hall of Fame library in Cleveland.

He has written several books, including *Les Paul: The Lost Interviews* and *The Day John Met Paul: An Hour-by-Hour Account of How the Beatles Began.*.

The Day John Met Paul has been published by Penguin in several languages, ranging from Japanese to Czech to French, and is available as an audiobook read by Rod Davis, a personal friend of John Lennon.

O'Donnell holds a Master's Degree from St. Peter's College and studied journalism under New Journalism pioneer Richard Goldstein at New York University. He has also completed graduate courses in Creative Writing and the Teaching of Writing at Harvard University.

He has appeared frequently on CNN Radio and has done many television interviews. His biggest TV moment came when he didn't appear on the screen at all, but rather had his name show up in a *Jeopardy* question. The contestant answered correctly for $400.

He is a member of the Authors Guild, the Society of Professional Journalists, and the National Academy of Recording Arts and Sciences.

Part I: Concert

The Freddie Mercury Tribute: Queen Hosts One of the Greatest Concerts In Rock History

APRIL 20, 1992 (LONDON)—Arrivederci, Mercury. Adios, Freddie. Sayonara. Auf Wiedersehen. Bene vale.

Whatever the language, and wherever spoken, the English rock band Queen tonight gave most of the planet Earth a chance to say goodbye to their singer Mercury (a.k.a. Farrokh Bulsara, Larry Lurex, Mr. Bad Guy, The Great Pretender).

Indeed, between 6 p.m. and 10:32 p.m., British Summer Time, with God, MTV, BBC 2, Fox Television, Radio One, K-Rock, 72,000 in-the-flesh ticket holders, you, me, and for all I know the (real) Queen looking on, Wembley Stadium here boomed with the finest rock 'n' roll toast since the day Elvis made that birthday record for his mother.

Billed as "The Freddie Mercury Tribute: A Concert for AIDS Awareness," and called "A Concert for Life," the high-stakes, multi-million-dollar, history-making extravaganza attracted an audience of about one billion. Which means that some Buddhist monk in Lithuania won't have to wait up all night to hear what songs Metallica played, and a guy who drinks his beer out of a can and is on a two-hour coffee break in Jersey City right now can check out George Michael's huge hoop earring.

Seven satellites beamed the event to over 70 countries, including the U.S., Europe, the Far East, South Africa and Australia. On this Easter Monday on which all rocky roads lead to London, more countries broadcast the show live than any pop music event heretofore. The satellite link-up also provided feeds *back* to Wembley Stadium of U2 in Sacramento, Cal., and Mango Groove in South Africa.

The media coverage was a low bow to a man—and a band—that the U.S. press has generally underrated and overlooked for two decades. With several of the greatest rock musicians in the universe paying Queen the ultimate tribute of their talent, the message zipped loud and clear across umpteen time zones and postal codes: Queen is a world-class band of primo talent.

It was a long-deserved triumphal moment for Queen, a day of laughter and tears and music and nostalgia and footsteps. But the day offered another message as well, and that was the importance of people becoming involved in the fight against AIDS. The 45-year-old Mercury had died on Nov. 24, 1991, of bronchopneumonia resulting from AIDS.

Paying far more than lip-service to the cause, the entire event was non-profit, with international TV rights, ticket sales, and merchandising contributing precious cash to help those with the disease. Millions of dollars are expected to flow from the concert.

As rock concerts go, all in all, the 80's had "Live Aid"; the 70's had the "Concert for Bangladesh"; the 60's had "Woodstock"; the 50's had the "Nineteen-Fifty-Six Elvis Presley, Anywhere."

And, I would submit, the 90's had "The Freddie Mercury Tribute: A Concert for AIDS Awareness."

It's a lead-pipe cinch that there will never be another day like it this century—or maybe next.

Since it was a super day in a big bowl, the event ought to have a Roman numeral after it, like Super Bowls do. Of the five decade-marking occasions above, I'd put this one somewhere between I and III.

I mean, on the premises—and in tip-top form— were people with names like Robert Plant and Roger Daltrey and Axl Rose and Elton John and David Bowie. Calling that kind of talent an "all-star lineup," as the press release here does, is like calling the Sistine Chapel an "all-right ceiling." If you owned Fort Knox, you couldn't pay for all that talent on one bill.

Along with the registered legends, there was a striking range of musical colors from the rock 'n' roll rainbow—an astonishingly balanced blend of styles and ages. Some performers were so young, relatively speaking, you wondered if they were doing the show as part of a requirement for becoming an Eagle Scout. A few of them probably had to show ID to get served at the Wembley Hard Rock Cafe that was backstage.

Still, both the young and the not-so-young, the howlers and the hummers, delivered the goods. They played out of a surreal web spun of a legendary band, a mythical stadium, a video-captured ghost, and several thousand long memories. Anybody without AAA-1 talent on that stage today would have stood out like a freshman in a beanie with a propeller on it.

In essence, the 272-minute concert wended its way into rock history because of the quality of the performances; the stylistic and age range of the performers; the financial contribution to international charities; the effort to raise awareness among the young about a relentless global epidemic; and the depth of sincerity of each performer's tribute: every single musician was proud to perform for Freddie Mercury . . . and so gave everything.

With all that said, the big discussion among many journalists right now is how—despite all that talent, legendary and otherwise—almost nobody even came close to filling Mercury's shoes. As a billion or so people click off their TV sets, and the 72,000 who thronged this stadium now file back home, many in the non-British press are baffled that just about no singer could match the winged voice of the winged-named vocalist.

I, for one, don't happen to see anything unusual about the sentence, "Almost no one could sing as well as Freddie Mercury today." If that's a news bulletin, then so is, "Two plus two equals four," "Water freezes at 32 degrees Fahrenheit" and "A horse will win the Kentucky Derby."

Maybe some press people didn't know it's virtually impossible for anyone in the business to sing as well as Freddie Mercury, but someone by the name of Elton John knew it. When he sang Queen's "Bohemian Rhapsody" tonight, he didn't even *try* to hit Mercury's notes. His policy toward the song was as hands-off as the Monroe Doctrine. Artist that he is, he knew very well that you don't play around with a classic. There was more chance of him chipping away at the *Pieta* than there was of him trying to improve upon—or even imitate—the singing of that song.

Actually, if most vocalists had tried to match Freddie Mercury note-for-note this evening, they would have gotten cut up worse than if they'd tried to ride a shark and sprung a nosebleed. It would have been as dangerous as making a U-turn on the New Jersey Turnpike. The best almost anyone could hope to be was peccable. Ninety-nine percent of rock singers on this particular planet wouldn't have a prayer if they tried to out-sing Freddie Mercury. David Bowie didn't try to this evening, and he even had a prayer: he knelt down and said "The Our Father."

Fact is, Mercury, the element, may be Number 80 on the Periodic Table, but Mercury, the musician, is closer to Number 8—probably higher—on the table of all-time great rock 'n' roll singers. That's not just *my* opinion, by the way: that's also the opinion of Roger Daltrey, a man who understands rock 'n' roll lead-singing and losing a bandmate in equal measure.

After the concert, I had to pick my way through a courtly gathering of rock royalty backstage. It had been a long evening of deep feeling and I wondered what this lead-singer—who had earlier sung Queen's "I Want It All"—had on the tip of his tongue about the lead-singer who was missing. In a voice thick with emotion, Daltrey told me:

"When we lost Freddie, we not only lost a great personality, a man with a great sense of humor, a true showman, but we lost probably the best, the really, the *best* virtuoso rock 'n' roll singer of all time. He could sing anything in any style. He could change his style from line to line and, God, that's an art. And he was brilliant at it."

Over the years, Daltrey inspired respect with his singing. Jim Morrison inspired mystery. Paul McCartney inspired affection. Janis Joplin inspired quest. Mick Jagger inspired lust. Bob Dylan inspired thought. Grace Slick inspired cool. Bruce Springsteen inspired faith.

But Freddie Mercury inspired awe. To see him in full throat—the bazooka-length microphone held with a lover's grip; the deep dark eyes giving him a boy-next-door demeanor (if you lived next door to a coffin in a cellar in Transylvania); the tendon cords popping out the sides of his neck like red springs; the voice hitting notes so high, they came out with ice caps on them—was to witness not just excellent ability, but epic.

Freddie Mercury didn't perform, he feasted. He used a microphone as if he were tasting wine out of it. He didn't *sing* rock 'n' roll, he decanted it.

His charisma was enormous. Charisma is the difference between a singer you wouldn't cross the street to see and a singer you'd cross an ocean to see. When Mercury took a stage, it was Gable beating down the door to Scarlett O'Hara's bedroom. When he got off the stage hours later, he left you with a dramatic yet subtle sense of cliffhanger, like the latest installment of a Dickens' novel heading into a foreign 19th Century port. Mercury was the precursor of stadium rock because it took stadiums to hold him. It got to the point where seeing him sing in anything smaller than stadiums would be like seeing Rembrandt paint fingernails.

As much as anyone who ever grabbed a microphone, Freddie Mercury was a trail blazer, a standard-bearer. He sang every form in the business—rock, pop, blues, country, soul, disco, opera—without disgracing any of them. Music loves to dance in the voice of a great singer and Mercury had a superlative voice—a voice so classical, you figured it was on touring loan from the Bettman Archive, the Smithsonian, or the Louvre. The guy had to stifle his sneezes because of the stained glass in his throat.

It was as if he didn't really "hit" notes: he would more or less *sweep* them. His voice could go from teddy bear to bear in a millisecond. For your average singer, the only way a throat could drop that suddenly would be if it fell through a trap door. Leave it that, as rock 'n' roll landmarks go, the Mercury voice had the range of the Matterhorn and the complexity of the Eiffel Tower.

Singing seemed natural to him. You got the feeling that if he hadn't been singing Wembley for a living, he would have been a singing waiter. Born Farrokh Bulsara in Zanzibar, raised in India, metamorphosed in England, beloved by millions, headed for immortality, he taught himself the arcane principles of singing. He was as obviously right for music as Pele was for soccer, Monroe for movies, Churchill for politics.

During his twoscore and five years on Earth, Mercury was often called "flamboyant." But his lifestyle would have had to have simmered down quite a bit before he could merely be called "flamboyant." Calling Freddie Mercury "flamboyant" is like calling *The Wizard of Oz* "nonfictional," or like saying the Johnstown Flood was "wet."

He was, by report, a man with a ripping laughter—a guy who said and did outrageous, eccentric, ostentatious, unpredictable, havocsome things. Mercury came on strong—had a character of many facets, and none of them dripped. He was one-of-a-kind, but not selfish. As Queen's field general, he didn't use his rock music skill as a self-glorifying *pas seul* that would lead to better things. Rather, like Jim Morrison before him, he was proud to be part of a rock 'n' roll team.

Not for nothing (and not just for rock 'n' roll senior citizens, either), think back to some rock masterworks and consider what they reveal about their creators. The Stones sent a red-hot sympathy card. Springsteen hit on running as a birthright. Dylan rolled back a stone and wanted you never to forget how it does *feel.* John Lennon just imagined. Zep climbed a stairway beyond the stars. Clapton pictured a guy on his knees and pleading.

No surprise, then, that Freddie Mercury rhapsodized bohemianly. 'Tis said he was magnificent to watch but impossible to figure out. No one could get a thermometer on Mercury. His bearing could go from Machiavelli to Mary Poppins in a finger snap; from *Lord of the Flies* to *Lilies of the Field.* He was reputedly as vain as Napoleon, yet as generous as Santa Claus.

In his life's work, he sang songs and performed shows and wrote music and lyrics just how he wanted to. He never sold out. There was more chance of seeing a "For Sale" sign on the *Mona Lisa* than there was of seeing one on Freddie Mercury. His lyrics—like his voice and stage show—unveiled stunning vision. The man's written words are about as different from most rock lyrics as broken English is from Queen's English. To listen carefully to "March of the Black Queen," for example, is to meet someone who knows more secrets than Merlin the Magician. The late singer's writing furnishes one more key facet of his blue-chip talent.

Blue-chip talent and blue-sky weather were the forecasts for Mercury's tribute this April 20 (or IV/XX) and both calls were on the money. Usually, for an event of this magnitude, the pre-concert worries center on logistics related to performers, equipment and crowds. But, this being Great Britain, the biggest worry was that it would rain on the Rock 'n' Roll Easter Parade. There was a good chance, in other words, that people would turn on the *television* channel and think they were seeing the *English* Channel. Instead of seeing a swan song, they would just see swans. I figured it was about a 70-30 chance I'd be wearing a wet suit to the gig and wind up filing a surfing piece. For my money, the wettest autumn I ever saw was a summer I spent in England.

As it turned out, we were granted that rarest of British commodities: a mostly sunny day. By 5 p.m., an hour before showtime, a small breeze was lazing its way through the superstadium known as Wembley. It was turning into a fine bright spring evening and Wembley's double domes gleamed like giant icebergs in a warm-blooded sea of humanity. The stadium makes most rock 'n' roll venues look like a phone booth. Wembley has become a classy showcase—rock music's Wimbledon. The last time Queen tunes bounced around here was 1986. But the place still drips with Queen memories. The band's music has stayed on the stadium seats like a coat of paint.

So it was not unexpected that Wembley would be the chosen site for this tribute. What *was* unexpected, at least to these eyes, was that Queen was attempting to do the show at all. What a daring endeavor: to bring back the spirit of Freddie Mercury for an encore! Given Queen's vast repertoire and Mercury's vast voice, trying to fit the man's career into one evening would be like trying to shoehorn Texas into a mud puddle in Maine.

This concert-tribute-party-benefit was on the drawing boards for five months. Six days after the lead-singer's death in November, Queen guitarist Brian May, one of the authentic gentlemen of rock, was already talking about it. "One of the things I would definitely like to do," May informed me, "is a memorial gig for Freddie. A lot of people have already told me that they would love to appear, you know, singers all over the world have said they would love to come and sing a song for him. Which I think would be just the way he would enjoy it: the biggest that's ever been done—the biggest and the best."

When May said those last words, a FASTEN YOUR SEATBELT sign lit up in my head. All I could think was that Queen had every intention of pulling out all the stops for their friend and bandmate of 20 years.

The day the tickets for tonight's show went on sale, the mad dash couldn't have been madder if they'd been tossing bales of money out of the Tower of London. There has been much media ballyhoo over the fact that the show sold out in three hours, and without any of the guest performers being announced. But Queen fans are a special breed: they didn't scoff up all 72,000 tickets in a wink for the guests; they scoffed up all 72,000 tickets in a wink for Queen.

You see, in politics, Queen means royalty. In rock 'n' roll, Queen means royalty AND loyalty. These are people who have cleaved to the band for much of their lives and marked important days in their lives by what Queen single or album had most recently been released. I've known fans of many bands and sports teams, and I'd say Queen fans are among the most loyal in the world. You tell Queen fans you're going to write a piece about their boys and they look bemused. You get the feeling they're certain that the only reporters who could possibly get the story right are named Matthew, Mark, Luke and John.

Today's show—Queen's last ever—was scheduled to start at 6 o'clock Monday night. Tickets for the *stands* had seat numbers on them; tickets for *the field* were on a first-come/first-in basis. To secure a spot near the stage, Queen fans started setting up camp outside the stadium at 6 o'clock *Sunday morning.* These were people who knew Queen's work, and respected it, and were willing to endure a 36-hour wait to be as close as possible to the band, or what was left of it.

The waiting ended, on schedule, and the wonder began. Framing the stage were two gargantuan-sized, kaleidoscopically-splashed towers. Both towers extended beyond the stadium roof. Next to the towers hung a couple of colossal video screens. At exactly VI o'clock, the speakers crackled, the lights lighted, the notebooks opened, the cameras pointed, the crowd cheered, the videotape spun, and the four sky-gazing faces of Queen's "Bohemian Rhapsody" video loomed up on the screens. The opening piano notes of the song drifted across Wembley's outsize acreage and warmed the crowd like a wave of sunripples.

The video proved to be a collage of mostly Mercury images. As it ended, the three Queen bandmates walked onto the stage, without their instruments, and faced the audience from behind three microphones, as if they were waiting for Alex Trebbek to fire the first *Jeopardy* question at them. The applause snapped from every nook and cranny of the stadium. Someone on the long flat field unfurled a banner that said: "Goodbye Freddie. We Will Love You."

Drummer Roger Taylor was exuding so much nervous energy, he seemed prepared for a decathlon, while bassist John Deacon stood there looking more like a certified public accountant than a certified rock star. Brian May, a guy so technically adept he could take a guitar apart while still playing it, told the crowd: "We are here tonight to celebrate the life and work and dreams of one Freddie Mercury. We're going to give him the biggest send-off in history!"

Roger Taylor's message to the crowd was "Cry as much as you like," and the words appeared to suit the band's emotional state. Maybe it was that this would be the first time the group ever took the stage without their lead-singer. Or maybe it was that this would be Queen's swan song. Or maybe it was just that the lighting was so good that it couldn't have gotten any better if they'd booked the show at the North Pole, but I thought the band's faces bore the signs of long emotional wear and tear. They looked hollow this Easter Monday, like chocolate Easter bunnies, ready to crack. They had every reason to crack, of course, having lost Freddie Mercury and then spending most of the next five months organizing this concert.

The concert was organized in two parts: the afternoon session and the evening session. The afternoon session featured performers doing mostly their own material. Included were three songs each by Metallica and Def Leppard; two songs by Guns 'n' Roses; a Queen medley by Extreme; and one song each by Bob Geldof and Spinal Tap. There were also the satellite feeds from California and South Africa, and a speech about AIDS from Elizabeth Taylor.

The evening session—the marrow of the concert—put forth Queen playing Queen songs with guest vocalists and some guest musicians. Singing three songs each were Robert Plant and George Michael; singing two songs apiece were Elton John, Lisa Stansfield, David Bowie, and Axl Rose; singing one song each were Roger Daltrey, Joe Elliott, Ian Hunter, Seal, Paul Young, Brian May, Zucchero, Annie Lennox, Gary Cherone, Liza Minnelli and James Hetfield. Guest musicians included Bowie on sax; Slash, Mick Ronson, Tony Iommi and Chris Thompson, guitars; Mike Moran, keyboards; and the London Community Gospel Choir, back-up vocals.

From the moment the first guitar riff pealed across the bright blue London sky, it was evident that this concert would be different in at least one important way. Since the man of the hour was a memory, not a man, the participants avoided the usual all-star-show gunslinging. That is to say, none of the musicians tried to push his reputation up a notch on the old six-string belt by out-playing someone else. There was interplay, not gun play. The guys of lesser reputations didn't try to challenge the fastest legends in the west. Everybody remembered they were in London, not Dodge City, and that it was a show for AIDS awareness, not ego-energizing, even if a mere billion people were looking on. They kept in mind that the movie helping to trigger the recent Queen Renaissance was called *Wayne's World,* not *John Wayne's World*

The World-At-Large heard Queen's John Deacon introduce a thrash-metal band called Metallica and the TV World was suddenly staring at a guy who looked back at them like he was making faces at a tiger. It was lead-singer James Hetfield doing a song called "Enter Sandman," all the while appearing so grizzled you could scratch a match on his forehead. Even his voice seemed to have fuzz on it. But, all the same, the band got the mammoth crowd jumping. By the end of the set, people were rhythmically punching the air over their heads. At one point, Wembley's Press Officer, Marty Corrie, took a long look at the crowd and said he'd never seen so many people on the field for any event.

Next up was a Boston funk-metal group called Extreme. Guitarist Nuno Bettencourt and his band blinked in wonderment that they were there. I had the feeling that, if they hadn't been asked to take part in this little picnic, they would have stood in line to buy tickets. Despite their admiration for Queen—or more likely because of it—Extreme pulled off the gutsiest move of the day: they played a medley consisting only of Queen songs, both electric and acoustic. Most bands would climb the Grand Canyon in high heels before they'd do a long medley of a famous group's tunes for that group's audience. There's always the extreme chance that the imitators will fall flat on their faces by not embodying the spirit of the songs *exactly right* for the band's followers.

But Extreme took the chance and went over big. The acoustic songs slid through the crowd like a fresh seabreeze. For the faster electric tunes, lead-singer Gary Cherone used youth and speed and gesture and energy and motion to deal with the hearts of Queen fans. He was all over the stage, running around like Charlie

Chaplin being chased by the cops. For the most part, Extreme seemed to feel as at home on Queen's turf as an Eskimo on a ski slope.

Between sets, while roadies changed band equipment, the audience was treated to video interludes on the big screens. The videos displayed a vigorous Freddie Mercury and his three rock 'n' roll brethren. During performance sequences—Mercury flashing sharp eyes like a circling eagle—the crowd would applaud and sing along. During interviews, the crowd became enraptured and quiet, so much so that at times the place sounded more like someone shuffling a deck of cards than like 72,000 people at a rock 'n' roll gig.

The third band in the show (a real band now, not a video) was Def Leppard, a British heavy-metal group. In three songs, lead-singer Joe Elliott took the crowd over like a blonde rooster in a giant barnyard. Bob Geldof, producer of 1985's Live Aid concert, then did a traditional Irish folk song he had written with Mercury. It's a good thing he was introduced before he came on because, in his sunglasses and sunflower-powered suit, he could have scared King Kong back up the skyscraper. With his homemade ditty (called "Too Late God"), he effectively played the audience as if it were an old upright piano.

Spinal Tap followed, executing the role of court jester on Queen's royal stage. They performed their "Majesty of Rock" segment as if it had been directed by P.T. Barnum, and treated their own presence at the show with all the seriousness of Bob Hope playing for a troop encampment at Christmas.

The afternoon session's last band, Guns 'n' Roses, didn't *capture* the audience: they *leveled* the audience. As Slash's lightning-rod guitar streaks road the afternoon breezes, lead-singer Axl Rose bolted around the stage like a raging bull. You didn't know whether to listen to him or fight him off with a cape and sword. I was glad I wasn't wearing red. He danced and whirled and roared and went knockin' on Freddie's door with a voice as ripping as a chain saw. Talk about being on the cutting edge! He left little doubt about why he's one of the foremost rock singers today.

As the afternoon shadows lengthened and the concert neared its halfway point, the next personage to be presented at court was (How's this for amazing garnish, Freddie?) Elizabeth Taylor. In America, there was outright shock that Queen got Liz Taylor for their stage. Most Americans who thought about it at all, figured they'd get Roseanne. After all, wasn't this the band that released an album in 1976 and got a congratulatory telegram from Groucho Marx?

Understand it or not in the other-worldly U. S. of A., here she was, the world's most famous queen of beauty, standing at a podium in England, to talk about the nastiest four-letter word in any country: AIDS. What she told the crowd, fundamentally, was to keep yourself alive. "You are the future of our world," she said. "You are the best and the brightest. You are the shining lights that will illuminate a better world tomorrow. Protect yourselves."

She was just building momentum when—*sacre bleu!*—some of the people in front, with all the manners of Krushchev at the U.N., started shouting at her. "Get off!" someone yelled. "Let's have some music!" hollered someone else—someone who sounded as if he had packed away more than his share of the 26,000 pints of beer consumed at Wembley this evening.

Apparently, a few people thought they could divorce her, so to speak, from the matter at hand. But it didn't happen. She stared and pointed toward the noisy area and said forcefully: "I'll get off in a minute. I'll get off. I have something to say." The crowd cheered and the speech continued without further interruption.

As the audience listened to Taylor under the darkening sky, I recalled reading that it was on a clear, calm April evening, exactly 80 years ago, that a ship called the *Titanic* sank in the North Atlantic. Since the ship was supposed to be "unsinkable," it was equipped with enough lifeboats for only half the passengers. So 1,595 people perished. As the ship sank, those lucky enough to make it to lifeboats could hear the band playing stoically. With tonight's AIDS warnings in mind, I reflected on how many music listeners in this sea of people might believe that their sexual lives are "unsinkable" . . . and won't take precautions . . . and will perish.

In actuality, the *Titanic* put up a better fight against sinking than a lot of people are putting up against AIDS. At least the *Titanic* knew it was in trouble. Most of the earth *still* hasn't figured that out so far as AIDS is concerned. There are people, at this moment, not protecting themselves and, in so doing, buying first-class, round-trip cruises on the

Titanic—maybe even applying for the position of ship Social Director.

I began to appreciate how Queen had split the focus of this concert in half. It wasn't just "The Freddie Mercury Tribute," but also "A Concert for AIDS Awareness." The band used this night to try to make brothers and sisters of all the people of the world—to create one family to fight this holocaustic disease. For people who left the stadium—or turned off their TVs—with a decision to be more careful because of AIDS, this concert was the most important four-and-a-half hours of their lives. Queen can't make it into the Rock 'n' Roll Hall of Fame yet because it hasn't been 25 years since their first record release. But their efforts to raise AIDS awareness and proceeds put them in a much bigger class, the Humanity Hall of Fame. Their humanitarian gestures would make them one of the greatest groups in the world, even if they'd never had a hit record, or the singer couldn't carry a tune.

Carrying the responsibility of bringing the concert to a Mercurial climax was the second-half session with Queen playing back-up to several vocalists who would sing Queen songs.

Twilight began to settle on England. The evening sun dappled the stadium with flecks of zodiacal light as the three bandmates kicked the concert into warp-drive. Admirably as they played, the trio seemed jangled to be performing without their missing friend. As the heavy-hearted musicians rocked before a heavy-lidded sun, I wondered about the thinking they were doing this night. I started wondering if *they* were wondering, in the mist of memory, how they'd ever arrived on this London stage, under a late sun, playing rock 'n' roll for a good slice of the so-called civilized world. Could it have really been as long ago as 1973 that Farrokh Bulsara, Brian Harold May, Roger Meddows Taylor and John Richard Deacon released an album called *Queen?*

And, alas, many critics promptly said the record wasn't worth making. The only guy who got attacked more than Queen that year for keeping a tape recorder going was Richard Nixon. The next year they came out with *Queen II.* The band knew it was up to something special: that's probably why they used a Roman numeral, like Popes do. One of the best albums of all time, the songs were highly poetic. The media's general response, in this case, was that the group had gone from bad to verse.

Thus were the beginnings of a band-press relationship that Dickens would have understood perfectly: Queen was having the best of times, and the press was calling it the worst of times. I have a theory that, in rock 'n' roll, *imitation* isn't the sincerest form of flattery: *abuse* is. They made Elvis put on a tuxedo and sing "Hound Dog" to a hound on network television—to a real-life basset hound. They booed Dylan at Forest Hills in '65 when he walked out on stage with an electric guitar. They put Jimi Hendrix on the same bill as the Monkees. They made the Stones change their lyrics for an *Ed Sullivan Show.* I ask you: where else but in the rock arena can you get inducted into a Hall of Fame that no one has yet been able to get around to building?

If abuse is flattery in rock 'n' roll, then Queen might just be the most flattered band in the history of the music. For a while, they all but cornered the dissed market. No rock band so great ever got so attacked. And no rock band so attacked ever got so great.

The central reason the band could stay so strong-minded was self-explanatory: each band member had a strong mind. First off, they were about as open to interference as the House of Habsburg. Secondly, this was one of the most well-schooled rock groups ever. Each of the musicians had a degree—as well as a pair of eyes that told you there was a mind in back of them working double-overtime-and-a-half.

This is the band that could appreciate a Shakespearean sonnet as much as an Easter bonnet. They know that the Trojan War isn't a corporate battle between condom companies. They think in cosines. They don't just play out of rhythm and blues, but logarithm and blues. The first thing guitarist Brian May did when he got a 16-track recording studio in his home wasn't an all-night-super-boogie-jam: he wrote the music for a theater production *of Macbeth.*

From the moment Queen first appeared as Queen at Truno City Hall, Cornwall, in June of '70, they had a terrible problem: they believed that music should be original and that it should be created only because the musicians felt like creating it. They believed, intrinsically, that rock 'n' roll should be fun. In one of rock's most endearing quotes, Freddie Mercury described Queen this way: "We're the Cecil B. DeMille of rock 'n' roll. We always want to do things bigger and better."

Queen's first stab at being "bigger and better" was to blend hard rock and harmony—to be as heavy as, say, Led Zeppelin, but as harmonious as, say, the Beach Boys. In attempting this oxymoronic yoking of seemingly disparate musical forms, the group developed a pulsating crystalline sound that had the gloss of high-finished marble. They didn't just write and record a song: they superstylized it. The finished product was defiantly original, and would stay that way.

All four musicians composed the songs and, as time went on, the band thrived on experimenting with new styles. "Bohemian Rhapsody," a song with more changes than a month-old baby, was covered by the London Symphony Orchestra and interpreted by the British Royal Ballet. "Another One Bites the Dust" spun its way into discos. "We Will Rock You" and "We Are the Champions" have become anthems on stadium loudspeakers in many nations. By not keeping to one style, Queen broke through a spate of musical boundaries.

Just as they wouldn't create and record by formula, the band also raised live-performance rock to a new standard. With their dry ice and stage lighting and catwalks and smoke bombs and stage sets, Queen practically invented stadium rock. In 1977, their live act tendered a 5000-lb. "crown" of lights. Fifty-four-feet wide and 26-feet high, the dazzling crown would lift and drop at the opening and closing of the performance, flashing like a royal spaceship. If the road-show stage sets had gotten much more elaborate, they would have had to do their tours on aircraft carriers and people would have to watch from the shore.

As for the performances themselves—apart from the stage rigging—Queen wasn't just superb: they were *routinely* superb. You had the feeling that this group regarded playing poorly as a hanging offense. Whether performing at the Ingliston Royal Highland Exhibition Hall in Edinburgh, or the Farm Arena, Harrisburg, Pa.—whether playing Tokyo or Toronto—this was a band that could charm a rope out of a basket, make a snake do "The Twist." At Live Aid in 1985, without a sound check let alone a 54-foot-crown light show, Queen couldn't have stolen the show any better if Mercury had a cutlass in his teeth and a jolly roger across his shirt. On a bill that included Sting, U2, Madonna and Neil Young, Queen was named best act of the day by the show's organizer, Bob Geldof, as well as by a TV audience poll.

Besides advancing methods of studio recording and concert performance, Queen also helped inaugurate the use of music video. Released in 1975, the "Bohemian Rhapsody" video was an unprecedented feat of sight-and-sound craftsmanship. The group continued to enhance the medium throughout their career. The most recent Queen video, *Innuendo,* was awarded the Gold Camera Award at the U.S. Film and Video Festival.

Instead of giving Queen the star treatment for such work over the past 20 or so years, many rock critics often just gave it the treatment. The first album in 1973 was critically affixed as just another Glam Rock entry in the Gary-Glitter-Marc-Bolan-Slade mold. During the course of Queen's first ten years of recording, the only year that a Queen album wasn't knocked, slammed, flayed and otherwise dragged over the coals was 1983—and that was because there was no Queen album that year.

From the outset, many critics thought the band was trying to be a Zep copy, pure and simple. So Queen became The-Band-That-Was-Not-Led-Zeppelin, rock's Hindenburg, and, critically, sunk like a flaming disaster. Because the songs were so well-produced, the group drew fire as being a soulless conglomerate that could only manufacture, not create. In rock music, rugged spontaneity supposedly signifies sincerity and so, conversely, polish is often taken to mean slick contrivance. On reconsideration, accusing this meticulous gold record band of being "too polished" was like accusing a meticulous gold medal Olympic runner of being "too fast."

Anyway, because the songs encompassed so many different styles, the group was accused of having no identity; the stage sets and dry ice and lighting effects were seen as too glitzy and farfetched—when actually they were far-sighted; that "oxymoronic yoking" of hard with harmony was viewed as simply moronic; putting out videos made them "hype" artists, not artists; Mercury's line about Queen being the "Cecil B. DeMille of rock" turned out to be more endooming than endearing: it was like saying "It's all showbiz"—the worst sort of blasphemy to those who believe rock 'n' roll is High Art. To purists, the line belonged right up there with Leo Durocher's "Nice guys finish last."

To most other people with ears upside their heads, it was plain that Mercury had the nerve to state the truth: at its root, rock 'n' roll *is* showbiz—it *is* an entertainment. Done well and originally, it can be art, too. But it has to be accessible and enjoyable. Queen knew that instinctively and that's why they went for *everything:* the overt showmanship, the artful videos, the painstaking production, the immense staging. *It wasn't that Queen was more interested in the show than the music—or more interested in selling than rocking. It was just the opposite: because the group cared so much about the music, they worked on the other stuff as a showcase to enrich the music, not to divert from it.*

Critical understanding of that particular idea—or of Queen as a band—was at its worst in America. In the 70s, the U.S. knew who you meant by John-Paul-George-and-Ringo, but wouldn't know Queen even if you gave out their *last* names. To most Americans, Mercury-May-Taylor-and-Deacon were a planet, month, job and church official, not a rock band. There were probably more Americans who could recite the Pythagorean Theorem than could tell you the names of the four guys in Queen. The only time you saw an American newspaper with the headline, "MERCURY CONTINUES TO SOAR," it was a hot day in mid-summer.

For many Americans who *had* heard of the band, it was considered rock 'n' roll's Loch Ness Monster: a mythical yet submerged creature of utterly unknown and vicissitudinous qualities. The main burr under the Queen saddle in the U.S. was some of the public's homophobic misreading of the band's name and image, and subsequent mishearing of the group's music. The band called itself "Queen" and the lead-singer was a guy wearing black fingernail polish, silk capes, eye make-up, tight jump suits and silver bracelets. The suspicion was that "Queen" was not just the name of the group, but a description of the band's sexual orientation. In the macho world of 1970's rock, such a stance would catch flak, to say the least.

Even so, Queen acquired an American following and would probably have prospered even more in the U.S. were it not for the 1984 release of a video called "I Want to Break Free." The video was a parody of a British soap opera, *Coronation Street,* and showed Queen's four musicians dressed in drag. While English viewers understood that it was a joke, American viewers did not. Still not altogether sure about the band's name and the lead-singer's taste in nail polish, many 1984 Americans deemed the video out-and-out hissable. It didn't help *extinguish* the homophobic fire in America: it poured gasoline on it. So far as Queen's "popularity" in America was concerned, it appeared at the time that they had sipped hemlock out of a pink slipper.

Fortunately, the yardstick for measuring greatness in rock 'n' roll is not steadfast world popularity and it's not critics. You are measured by the original quality of your work. And they don't come down the road much more original than Queen. Critics who kept attacking the group might as well have gone up a mountain and shouted "Stop it!" at their echoes. For two decades, despite the underwhelming support of America in the mid-to-late 80's, the music just kept on coming. In England, Queen stayed as popular as the Queen. In fact, for the past couple of decades,

Buckingham Palace has been getting a good deal of the band's fan mail by mistake.

With dedication, patience, fortitude and perseverance, Queen established itself as not just a great band, but a tough one. Today, there is a long-long-long-long overdue Queen Renaissance internationally. The myths about the group and the reality of the group have reached a media flashpoint. What's cutting through the heat of that flash and finally putting the reality before the public's eyes, of course, has been the inclusion of the "Bohemian Rhapsody" video in the *Wayne's World* movie. Millions of young people—people who weren't even born when Queen began—are picking up on, and buying, Queen albums. These are people for whom Queen isn't an acquired distaste. They're just listening and liking what they hear—no image problems or critical onslaught or anything else about it.

How oracular that Queen's first single was "Keep Yourself Alive": the band has had to make a career of that enterprise. It takes a certain generosity of spirit to make a marriage or a friendship work, and it's the same thing with rock bands. It is that spirit which makes a band a team, instead of a motley of musicians, and Queen had it. In point of fact, Queen has been a band of generous spirit in many ways. Not only are all the proceeds of tonight's benefit going to charity, but four days ago the group donated $1.76 million to the Terrence Higgins Trust, an English charity for AIDS sufferers. The money was from the royalties earned on the re-release of "Bohemian Rhapsody" on CD. Also, Queen has raised millions for the British Bone Marrow Donor Appeal. The organization assists children dying of leukemia or related diseases. That kind of generosity tells the story of what the group Queen is about, tells it even better than a glance at their accomplishments, record-setting as they were.

Under the setting sun of a Monday evening in London, the surviving Queen musicians began the part of the show that the fans had been waiting for. The three bandmates played their instruments as they've played them scads of times in concert before. Roger Taylor turned his drumset into a musical launchpad, playing so hard he probably developed second-degree burns on his fingers. John Deacon, looking clean-cut as a Disney movie, hammered out his dependably solid basslines. Brian May generated his customary ultra-precise sounds, not so much by *playing* the guitar as *operating* on it: Brian Surgery. And, as usual, the fans listened intently to that guitar, as if mesmerized by a crackling fireplace.

The three musicians played their songs, made their moves, did their jobs, and the sound rang loud and tight and upbeat. But there was that one thing different and it showed in their faces throughout the night: that wasn't their bandmate at the center-stage microphone. Hard as they would play, cheerful as they would try to look, Wembley Stadium's 5000 stage lights caught the emotional sunset in their faces. At times, they seemed to be looking straight ahead at something no one else could see. It was as if they were listening for footsteps.

Stepping into Freddie Mercury's shoes to pitch Queen music into the invading night was a veritable galaxy of starry voices. Elton John—rock's "Iron John": a fellow who has spent his lifetime with

crowds looking up at him—demonstrated his
sensational skill with "The Show Must Go On."
Roger Daltrey, brandishing his smoldering blue eyes
and whiplashing the microphone cord over his head,
was fabulous on "I Want It All." George Michael,
his chin capped in the usual piece of #4 sandpaper,
was in overpoweringly good voice on his three
songs, especially "Somebody to Love." David
Bowie, the Man Who Fell to Earth, sang two songs
in his ever-amazing way, then fell to one knee, bowed
his head, and recited "The Our Father." The prayer
cut into the audience's heart like a Bowie knife.

Axl Rose, careening left and right like he was in
a canoe race, scorched his lungs to deliver an
astounding rendition of "We Will Rock You."
Earlier, he had teamed up with Elton John and the
duo tried valiantly to do justice to "Bohemian
Rhapsody." When they crossed arms at the end of the
song, it looked less like a sincere joining of limbs
than an amateur pickpocket practice.

The night came quickly, tossing billions of
microscopic blue coins upon the stadium. As the
evening darkened, the mood of the crowd deepened.
The feeling of celebration gradually changed to one
of remembrance. Eyes adjusted imperceptibly to the
night light, and minds adjusted imperceptibly to the
actual reason for this gathering—a death.

Nowhere was this sense of loss more
heartrendingly aroused than in Brian May's solo
performance of "Too Much Love Will Kill You."
Sitting at keyboards, his voice seeming to weep, his
eyes blinking away tears, the gentle guitar giant gave
a memorable, soul-stirring performance. Every inch

of him seemed to feel both the beauty and the pain of what he was doing. Every time his eyes swept the stadium, they were moist. He was so misty-eyed by song's end, rollicking Wembley must have looked to him like a wobbly Noah's Ark.

As one Queen tune after another swelled the indigo English air, the clear day turned into a night of tangled feelings. For fans who measure time by rock 'n' roll memories in general, and Queen music in particular, it was like looking at a tree you had planted 20 years ago, and realizing the tree house you had built in it was gone. Yet, in the meanwhile, it was a charm to watch Paul Young do "Radio Ga Ga" and tap the audience like he was tapping a keg of beer; Lisa Stansfield, in hairnet and curlers and vacuum cleaner, camping it up in "I Want to Break Free"; Annie Lennox, looking like an eye-shadowed rabbit that had put all her Easter eggs in one basket, having a ball with David Bowie doing "Under Pressure"; George Michael and Lisa Stansfield leaning toward each other on "These Are the Days of Our Lives," as if they were Hansel and Gretel inspecting the oven; Ian Hunter, a man of self-containment, leading all the not-so-young dudes on "All the Young Dudes."

The performance highlight of the day most surely belonged to Robert Plant. A sterling talent commensurate with the tribute's cynosure, Plant was absolutely brilliant as he sang "Innuendo," broke into "Kashmir," then finished "Innuendo." Plant evoked a velvety blue presence under the crisp London evening that was twinkling overhead. He was a shimmering sapphire in a stadium-sized white ring.

With the glinting microphone as his lamp, he played Aladdin and sent forth a rock 'n' roll genie of entrancing power. His voice prowled the upper floors of "Innuendo" and "Kashmir" like a cat burglar. Then he sang "Crazy Little Thing Called Love" and his stage persona gripped and galvanized the crowd in a manner that kindled memories of the Mercury fire. Plant closed his set by singing the Led Zeppelin song, "Thank You." With May standing next to him during the tune, it looked like New York's Twin Towers had been hijacked across the Atlantic and snow-capped with brown ringlets. As the two rock veterans joined in the majestic song of thanks, a fresh breeze rolled through the cavernous stadium and fingered their heartbreaker curly hair. The crowd swayed in time to the tune and, as Plant wrapped up, sent its applause rolling toward the stage in bursts of rock 'n' rolling thunder.

For the socko three-handkerchief finale, it was all hands on deck for the last sail of the good ship Queen. The pantheon of performers melted into a single chorus line to back up Liza Minnelli—a princess of the Queen court because Freddie Mercury had often cited her as an influence. "There's one person Freddie would've been proud to have stand in his footsteps," said Brian May as he introduced Minnelli.

Just about the entire cast joined arm-in-arm to give the fallen star their final accolade. It was to be a rendition of "We Are the Champions," a sort of "My Way" the rock 'n' roll way. With Minnelli in

Mercury's spot, she milked the song for all it was worth: Dairy Queen. The arm-linked rank of superstars rocked in cadenced unison, smiling wide to soften the hard fact of farewell, trying not to see Mercury's footsteps fading up into a sky that had turned into a giant pane of smoked glass.

But there they went. As the song floated upward, so did the Mercury footsteps. Not one of the 19 all-access TV cameras picked it up, nor did the guy at Mount Palomar's telescope, but there went Freddie Mercury—a sawed-off microphone in his hand, voice in high register, his eyes full of fantastical devilment, winking over his shoulder. There he went, fading away from the splendid lantern of a stadium to join the choir of Presley and Morrison and Joplin and the rest. Because of Queen's munificent gesture of this concert, millions of people were finally ready to let him go.

I'm beginning to think that while passion is rock 'n' roll's visible poetry, *com*passion is its invisible virtue. As I looked from the sky back to the stage, I focalized on the three bone-tired, soul-tired Queen musicians, smiling through their pain—professionals to the very end. I thought about how much easier it would have been for them to come to grips with their bandmate's death privately, quietly, simply. But instead they chose to give a billion people the chance to share their grief. With their colleagues and fans, Queen brought a friend home, and wished him good night. In the process, they made the trip an awareness-raising, eye-opening experience that might give many the gift of life. Even the *timing* of the concert bespoke thoughtfulness: the Easter Season, a period of hope after a time of hardship.

Can you imagine how much Freddie Mercury would have loved all this? At a show in his honor, David Bowie said "The Our Father"; Axl Rose and Elton John did a duet; Liza Minnelli sang her heart out; and Elizabeth Taylor got the longest speaking part. My guess is that what he would have loved even more was seeing his band welcomed into rock's front ranks, which was where it belonged all along. For as much as a concert, the night was a coronation: Queen now finally seen as worldwide champions, publicly entering the realm of rock royalty.

With all the remarkable ramifications of this wondrous day in olde England, the one that struck me most profoundly was the genuine affection that Brian May and Roger Taylor and John Deacon had for Freddie Mercury. By night's end, their hurt eyes were mute yet glorious testimony that the greatest gift they ever had in their lives was working with each other in a band called Queen. It wasn't just a singer or a musician or an entertainer or a star or a legend that they were mourning. No, at heart, the three men of Queen were sending a special message to the world about the winged-voiced messenger named Mercury.

And the message was that—come closer—Freddie Farrokh Bulsara Mercury had something bigger and better than sold-out stadiums and incredible talent and gold records: true and lasting friends.

Au revoir, Freddie. Ciao. Aloha. Godspeed.

Cheers. So long.

And, as that glimmering Led Zeppelin vocalist so exquisitely sang it, "Thank You."

Part II: Interview

A Guitarist Recalls His Singer: Brian May on the Death Of Freddie Mercury

NOV. 30, 1991, LONDON—The words dropping from his lips slowly and softly, like fresh roses dropping on an open grave, Queen guitarist Brian May this evening gave his first interview since the death of his lead-singer, Freddie Mercury, six days ago. The 45-year-old Mercury died at his home in London on November 24 of bronchopneumonia resulting from AIDS.

"I was numb the first night after it happened," said a grief-stricken May. "We all met and talked and I couldn't even cry. Then the next day I fell to pieces completely; couldn't do anything; crying.

"It has come and gone ever since," said the top-flight guitarist who has referred to Queen as a "family" in many interviews over the years. "There has been a part of me that was expecting it, and then there's a part of me that still gets completely knocked to pieces.

"It's a big thing. It's like all your adult life is over. It's irrational, but it feels that way, losing your best mate. It's just a major, major hurt."

Certainly, Freddie Mercury was a major, major force in a major, major rock group. With bandmates May, Roger Taylor and John Deacon, the rhapsodically bohemian lead-singer propelled Queen to worldwide record sales of over 80 million during the band's 20-year career. In the studio, the group's trademark was meticulous production work on richly varied material that ranged from hard rock to soft ballads.

The lyrics ran the spectrum from Late Punk to Early Kubla Khan. Queen's song, "Bohemian Rhapsody," was voted the Best Song of the last 25 Years by the British Phonographic Industry, and the 1975 video of the tune is considered a pioneering work.

On the road, the group often proffered its sound and fury to audiences that were the size of some small countries. Queen's touring technology consistently made pre-existing in-concert communication seem about as modern as carrier pigeon. One of the band's numbers, "We Are the Champions," has become a stadium anthem around the world. Like Dilsey in William Faulkner's *The Sound and the Fury,* Queen proved durable and lasted.

Given such an extraordinary track record, one would have expected that the Queen singer's last days would have been graced with the most royal of red-carpet treatment. But because of escalating rumors about his health, Freddie Mercury's last days were anything but regal.

"The last three weeks of his life, when he was in his house," says 44-year-old Brian May, "were made a total misery because there was always conjecture going on. The press was outside his house 24 hours a day. So he was literally kind of hounded toward his death. And I think if he'd made his announcement earlier that he had AIDS, all of that would have happened much earlier.

"There was certainly a feeling in this country, prior to this," continues May, "that if you weren't gay and you weren't promiscuous and you weren't some other things, then why worry? But it's amongst us. The plague is amongst *all* of us. There's no hiding away now.

"It was a great decision to admit to having AIDS," says May of his friend and singer who, on the day before he died, revealed he was suffering from the disease. "Freddie has given us such an incredible weapon by announcing it himself, rather than posthumously. It would have been so easy to write 'pneumonia' on the death certificate or be vague about it. But in actually saying he had AIDS, it has already started to make a huge difference in this country.

"The AIDS testing centers have seen a massive rise in the amount of people who want to be tested. Also, the Terrence Higgins Trust has been completely swamped with donations. The trust is the biggest organization in this country that provides for people who are suffering from AIDS who don't have proper care. And Freddie has donated a large part of his will to them.

"So the fact that he said it so clearly," says May, "has increased awareness in this country by a huge amount. He'd achieved all that he could achieve in his music. The time was right for the announcement. I think he made a wonderful, dignified exit— something to be proud of."

May's declaration of frankness as a weapon in the war against AIDS is backed up by Dr. Patrick Dixon, director of AIDS Care Education and Training in

England. Dr. Dixon believes that young people will take the disease more seriously not when they hear about statistics, but when they see its effects on real people.

Besides promoting AIDS awareness and subsequent prevention, May, the father of three, suggests that Mercury's example will also help open up sexual discussion on all levels: "I have a feeling," he says, "that Freddie's life and death will be even more pivotal than seems apparent at the moment. In this country, the fact that he was loved so much by men and women, quite openly, in public and in private— it's easier to talk about all this because of him.

"I find myself much more able to talk about the whole business of people's attitudes to sexuality quite freely," says May, who has a B.Sc. Degree in physics and is close to completion of a Ph.D. in astronomy. "My lady friend, Anita, put it very succinctly. She said, 'I think it's time for us *all* to come out of our closets.' You know?

"We *all* have various problems with our sexuality," the guitarist continues. "I think the time has come to stop being ashamed of anything like that, you know, and stop looking at people and trying to make out how they're different, and in some ways should be ashamed of how they feel.

"For me, I've had plenty of problems with my heterosexuality, and Freddie had problems with his homosexuality, and he dealt with them incredibly well, in a way that I'm very proud of. So I don't find it hard to talk about that stuff anymore. I just think we're all what we are and there's no reason to be ashamed of any of it. We just face it the best way we can."

Asked how long Mercury had AIDS, May answered: "That's something even I don't know the truth about. But I know it was a long time. The guys he was living with—they definitely were keeping it a secret for five years or so. It was his fondest wish that we should go on absolutely as if nothing had happened."

The veteran Queen guitarist explained why Mercury had waited until the eve of his death to disclose his condition: "I think that by *not* talking about it—even though that was hard for all of us—we were able to carry on and do what we do without interference.

"If it had been announced," says May, "then there would have been all this association with AIDS, and there'd have been kind of a sympathy vote. And you'd say: 'Well, why are people buying the records? Is it out of pity?' All that sort of stuff. What he gave us was to be able to carry on with music for music's sake, normally, as a full, healthy, functioning unit. Which is wonderful, really. I think maybe the last five years would have been a lot different, otherwise.

"It has been very hard for us," continues May. "All these things about 'Doesn't Freddie want to tour?' and all that sort of stuff. I mean, everybody obviously now understands what was going on, you know, particularly with regard to America.

"We decided to postpone doing America until things took the upswing. Then when signs came that there were no upswings, we couldn't do it, and I wasn't able to say that at the time, but I can say it now. You know it wasn't that Freddie didn't *want* to tour. He *couldn't*. And I think everyone can fully understand that now. But this has been going on a long time."

The gentle-voiced May went to great lengths to cut through his grief and cut down the Mercury image shot across the world recently as an over-indulgent, super-pretentious, self-centered prince of pomp.

According to the fellow who played guitar beside Mercury and circled the globe with him for two decades, the singer was a generous, hard-working man of immense talent.

"The Freddie I know," says Brian May, "was not a promiscuous man and he was not overcome by drugs and he was not as difficult as many people portrayed him. He was actually very generous to anyone who came close to him.

"He was generous in respect of giving credit and sharing responsibility and accolades. He was generous enough with us in a way that many lead-singers are not. You know, the lead-singer gets kind of thrust into the limelight. But Freddie was always very careful to share it with us.

"He sang, literally, as long as he could stand. He sang till he dropped, like he said he would. He worked on the last two albums, at least, under great difficulty."

In delineating Mercury's two-decade role in Queen, May established that, to him, the man who sang "We Are the Champions" was a "Champ" in every way:

"He was very inspiring, totally inspiring. He was the classic focal point for a group. Music came from different places between the four of us. But on stage he was the perfect channel through which we flowed towards the audience and back again. He was an incredible link.

"Even in the stadium gigs that we were doing towards the end, he could get right to the back and make people throughout the place feel as if he could communicate directly with them. He had an amazing gift for it. He was a total one-off and totally irreplaceable."

When it came to direct communication, Queen played for over six million people in 28 countries, and its fans are among the most loyal in the world. For them, there isn't enough confetti in the city of New York to give their boys a morning shower.

In terms of Queen's future, May was reminded that Robert Plant had once said that Led Zeppelin didn't exist from the moment their drummer John Bonham had died.

"I always thought that inside," said May. "I had the words rehearsed inside me to say that. Because we had always agreed—we'd talked about it many times— that if something happened to one of us, we always said that's the end if one of us goes.

"My feeling is that obviously we could never go out and be Queen, under that name, in the same way, without Freddie. It's unthinkable. And yet the fans are saying, you know, 'We would like something. We expect something. We don't want to lose you.' So we're thinking very carefully about what we actually *can* do. It's just going to take a little while to sort out.

"There's quite a lot of stuff on tape," continues May, whose gentlemanly air belies a musician whose heat-packing guitar solos are holy terrors. "We were halfway through the next album. I'm not quite sure how many tracks, finishable, we have. It has to be three or four, at least.

"And then there are many other bits and pieces we'd just started. So we have to make a decision on what we'll do with all that stuff. There are many, many, probably dozens of scraps of things that we've started. So we'll have to try and figure out what to do with it all. I'm concerned that there will be no dilution in the quality of Queen's work."

One Queen project appears firm, however, and that's a tribute concert. "One of the things I would definitely like to do is the memorial gig for Freddie, which I think would be great," says May. "I'm not quite sure what form it would take.

"A lot of people have already told me that they would love to appear, you know, singers all over the world have said they would love to come and sing a song for him. Which I think would be just the way he would enjoy it: the biggest that's ever been done—the biggest and the best. That would please him.

"I'm absolutely sure that what Freddie wanted was for us all to bounce on. There's no doubt about that. I think it would be counter-productive to just sit back and mope."

The ringlet-haired guitarist's words sink to a near-whisper as he remembers the friend he lost less than a week ago: "There's a flood of great memories in my mind and they're blocked up with grief at the moment. Every time I see his face, it's forming his wicked, kind of impish smile, and that actually makes me feel much closer to tears than some of the other stuff.

"You know, when you think of the good bits, that's when you get really affected and you can't speak and a lump comes to your throat. I can just see him kind of laughing."

The only time May's voice perks up during the interview is when the subject turns to the British Bone Marrow Donor Appeal. The organization helps children dying of leukemia or related diseases and May has helped raise millions for the cause. The appeal has already saved the lives of many children.

"I'm thrilled with how that's going," purrs the man who can make a guitar purr. "That's the biggest reward you could have."

Not surprisingly, Mercury's last words to May sang of outrageous wit. The guitarist's first solo studio album is due out in May, and his first solo single was recently released in England. When Mercury's condition began to deteriorate, May began to feel uncomfortable about turning out product while his bandmate of 20 years was confined to bed.

Explains May: "I was a little upset about the timing of my record. It had taken me all of these years to get something together. Then it was already about to hit the shops in England, my solo record, when he was just about to go.

"And I started to feel worried because I felt like it was a tasteless thing to have a record out while this was happening to him. I didn't want to go out and be grinning on a stage and performing when he was slipping away. I felt really bad about it.

"Well," continues May with a sigh, "the last quote from Freddie that came to me was actually through our manager. I'd seen Freddie the previous day, but hadn't realized how close it all was.

"And our manager was there the next day, and he said to Freddie: 'Look, Brian's a bit worried and he feels like it might hurt your feelings or it might not be the best time to have all this stuff happening.'

"And Freddie said: 'Don't be stupid, darling, it's the best publicity you could have.' So right to the end he was able to maintain his sense of humor, even knowing that he was probably not going to last the weekend."

The anguished Queen guitarist made it a point to express his appreciation for the support of the band's legions of fans during a difficult time in his life. "Everybody has been wonderful," said May from behind the soft, manor-house eyes. "More and more, the message is coming home, from all around the world, how dearly loved was Freddie Mercury."

Printed in Great Britain
by Amazon